Spiritual Travelers:

LIFE'S JOURNEY FROM THE PAST TO THE PRESENT FOR THE FUTURE

Ann Marie Ruby

ISBN: 0692846417
ISBN-13: 978-0692846414

www.ingramcontent.com/pod-product-compliance
Lightning Source LLC
Chambersburg PA
CBHW031958040426
42448CB00006B/402

DEDICATION

With the windmills blowing in the air retelling stories from the past to the present awaiting the future generation, tulips blooming from beneath the Earth, Holland stands in my eyes as a holy land. As She brews race, religion, and color into one, She calls Herself Holland.

Dreams haunted me as they landed upon my door. There was a fisherman's village where I kept finding myself. I knew there was a flood somewhere and everything was flooded. Again, I saw myself at a different place, this time near a castle, which had a moat and a bridge. Never in my life had I heard of these stories nor had I wanted to look into them out of fear. What if my dreams came to reality? All these dreams stayed with me for years until one night a strange dream haunted again. This time, a person knocked on my door.

I asked him, *"Who are you?"*

He said, *"Oh I am Mark, Mark Rutte."*

I asked, *"I never met you?"*

He said, *"No."*

I asked, *"You are a president?"*

He said, *"Yes, you can call me that. I am a Prime Minister."*

I said, *"Oh you are Tony Blair, Prime Minister Tony Blair?"*

He laughed and said, *"No. That was a few years ago. I am Mark Rutte and I work for the..."*

I stopped him and said, *"You work for the Queen."*

He said, *"I used to, but now I work for the King. Prime Minister Mark Rutte."*

As I woke up from this dream, I knew it was a knock on my door. For the first time without fear, I looked into my dreams and did the research. I got the biggest shock. I felt feverish as in front of me on the computer there was Prime Minister Mark Rutte from the Netherlands. History showed me there were floods in the Netherlands. There is a place called the fisherman's village. There is a port in Rotterdam which was a shock because I saw in another dream I live in the sister port city of the country that haunts me in my dreams. I live in Seattle, and the sister port city is Rotterdam in the Netherlands. I don't know how I ended up here, but I know I was there in my dreams.

Maybe one day, life will tell me how. In the meantime, I found this leader whom I have never met. Through my research, I was inspired by his quotes and the remarkable way he lives his life. Don't fear the past. Don't let fear knock you out. He teaches as he is a teacher and a historian. Without him knowing, he has taught me a lot.

I had always thought life is a circle. But, I learned he believes life is not a circle. He believes you complete the circle. As I kept reading about him, I understood what an honorable man he is. He believes in history as a lesson and guidance, but you create your own path. You create your own history. He teaches all humans should have equal rights. This historian goes and sits with Muslims, walks with Hindu and Jewish leaders, visits the Pope, and still believes all people regardless of their faith, religion, or race, deserve the right. All this time, I realized despite living in this century, I am an old soul and my dreams guided me to another who lives like an old soul.

Life is simple. Give the gift of kindness. Try to give and even though your gift might not be appreciated, in time, the future generation will be guided through your gift. I live not to be appreciated, but my soul wants to see the future generation being guided through my words.

Words are my soul and the wisdom I live for. Mahatma Gandhi inspired me from the past and Prime Minister Mark Rutte inspires me from the present. I know with time, all of this shall again be the past, but I wanted to frame my thoughts, my words of inspiration into a book. I began writing my thoughts for others who have been knocked out or those who need just a word or line to get back up and complete the journey they were born to take, for each one of us has a reason to be born.

Sometimes, we feel we have no reason to be here or get up in the morning, see the sun rising, or the sun setting for we let our depression take over. But, word of advice from one who has been there, there is tomorrow. For me, there is always today. Until today is over, I keep on living for one day I shall be history. But, I want my words to be there for you as a great man's word started my journey and gave me hope to continue the journey of my life.

My life journey is a wagon filled with struggles from all aspects of life. I take all of these as a traveler's journey of endurance. Life brings along this path inspiration from all different corners. My corner was an amazing grace from The Holy Spirit. Through my dreams, I was guided by The Holy Spirit and that path brought me to a stranger, a leader of a small European country known very well for his own journey and simple ways of life.

Sometimes in life, a person leaves a great imprint on one's soul, even though you may have never met. In my life, this person was Prime Minister Mark Rutte, who without knowing inspired this old soul.

From his inspiration, I find inspiration for all of you. I never met him personally, but I feel I know him through simplicity and his wisdom. From a faraway land, he has inspired this unknown person and may I an unknown person inspire you.

I call this book, *Spiritual Travelers: Life's Journey From The Past To The Present For The Future.*

Mark Rutte, The Historian, The Teacher, was my inspiration and for this, I dedicate this book to His Excellency Mark Rutte, Prime Minister of the Netherlands.

INTRODUCTION

Life is a journey all humans embark upon. This journey takes us through obstacles, pleasures, achievements, and disappointments of life. We are the travelers who have this journey upon us. Through time and tide, we must choose our turns of life. As the corners come upon our route, we choose our ways and sometimes it is then we need help from even strangers whom I call Angels in disguise.

Words are so powerful, they create or break a relationship. For me, words are the soul of my spirit. Words placed in a sentence create prayers, poems, and stories from the past, present, and future.

My inspirational quotations are my prayers for all. I have written these inspirational quotations for all traveling through the tunnel of life. May my words be the healing winds of life and give all the helping hand to stand up and keep strong.

Our journey continues as the travelers we are, *Spiritual Travelers: Life's Journey From The Past To The Present For The Future*.

THE TRAVELERS

I the traveler walk upon my journey.

The heated sun burns, blazing my skin.

The cold shivering chills of the freezing nights

Blister my skin.

I still am glad for I know this pain is nothing

For I have the glad tidings of my Lord

On This Path.

This Path, The Path to Heaven is all I want.

I see many travelers on the journey

Whom I bump into along the way.

Busy they are with the pleasures of life.

Women and men find comfort in each other,

Hiding from the cold nights as a one night stand.

People missing work for

They want to escape the blazing sun.

Escape you may today from the fire and cold,

But tomorrow at The Lord's House,

You shall burn and freeze eternally.

I teach them my Lord along the way,

Give glad tidings to your Lord and walk upon

His Road even though hard it may seem.

For this hardworking Road

Will take you to The Eternal Peace.

On The Road of The Lord,

You will find your true blessings.

These blessings may come hard,

But will take us to our Final Destiny.

The traveler I am, seeking to please my Lord.

Sacrifice I commit is but all my love for my Lord.

No sacrifice is but a sacrifice

For my Lord has a House ready upon my arrival,

Where no fire shall burn me,

Nor cold shall touch me,

Nor any misery shall befall.

For my Lord has The House ready

For those of us whom make the journey,

THE TRAVELERS.

*From my prayer book, *Spiritual Songs: Letters From My Chest*.

A DAY IN MY LIFE:
Ann Marie
Back From Heaven

Seattle is a city full of life where strangers say, "Hello," walk, and smile as if we are the best of friends, helping hands all around, never a dull moment. I had a strange encounter with a stranger, who had stopped and just said, "So Ann Marie, how does it feel to be back from Heaven?" I was shocked how he knew my name, not in his question.

I walked past him without uttering a word, but the words stayed with me. I believe in reincarnation and that life is a circle, but also believe this life has been given so we complete the circle, not let the circle complete us. Change what has been wronged and not be wronged. Some words linger on and just stay with you forever, for me these words of a stranger.

Words said are gone like the winds of time and tide. May we not throw out whatever comes to our mind, but always be of a helping hand, through our words and actions. Words are the prayers I live for. Words are the most powerful tool we were gifted with. Use them wisely as even with time, life becomes history, but words remain forever.

So, I give you words from my heart to yours, my inspirational quotations.

SEVEN DAYS OF INSPIRATION

Monday brings all creation back to reality, after all, life goes on.

Tuesday is for you and me as we all complete this journal of life.

Wednesday is hope giving day for all humans to stay involved with positivity.

Thursday is for all of whom are seeking the knowledge of guidance.

Friday the nights are always darker, but dawn is around the corner.

Saturday on this day let us give back to nature what she gives us without being asked.

Sunday even for one day and one night, may we the creation remember The Lord, as The Lord watches over us for eternity.

"*Close* your eyes
and see the love
spread throughout
this globe and as
it lights up each
and all houses,
may we open
our eyes and
realize this was a
dream, but now
it is a *reality*."

Quotation #1

"*Life* is about giving and *enjoying* the true gift of *giving*."

Quotation #2

"*I* will have peace as my support, *learn* to love *life*, and give the *gift* of *kindness*."

Quotation #3

"*Love* and union give birth to a *heart*. War and *hatred* break a *heart destroying* all around. *Spread* love and *peace*."

"*Realization* dawned *upon* me. *Nothing* is a *sacrifice*, as I devote my *life* to *peace*."

Quotation #5

"*Even* when they hate, you spread *love*, and maybe *one* day this *world* will have *peace,* joy, and *harmony*."

Quotation #6

"*I* struggled to stand up for *myself* first, *for* I know it is *then* I can stand up for *you*. Each blessed day I learn to *be* there for *myself* first as that is the *only* way I *can* be there for you *too*."

Quotation #7

"*Let* us be one world with one *boat* where we can *pick* up all of whom need *help* and those *of* whom do not *know* yet, but *also* need a *boost*."

Quotation #8

"*Let* us spread love throughout this *world* faster than *hatred*. *Violence*, hatred, and *racism* against any *being* should never be *tolerated*."

Quotation #9

"*Stand* up with me.
Help yourself first.
Then, as *we* hold
hands together, we
can help each *other*
as we *end* all
violence, hunger, *and*
war."

Quotation #10

"*The* time
we have during
these cold winter
nights, hold on
to the prayers and
hope, for with hope,
dreams are seen and
made. From dreams,
we have new
beginnings."

Quotation #11

"*Spread* love from each individual *house* and *make* this *Earth* one home for all *children.*"

Quotation #12

"*The* land, the sky, and all of this nature stand still, for all that moves is the human. The Artist of the canvas, and the true beauty of The Lord remain steadfast always there, for me today, and you *tomorrow*."

Quotation #13

"*The* awakening *realization* dawned upon me, by *giving up* something, I *gained* so much *more*."

Quotation #14

"*Race*, religion, color, even languages *are* all *blind* when and where, there is *love*."

Quotation #15

"*Let* us spread love and may *all* the negativities *be* erased from this *Earth,* our *Mother* Earth, we all *love.*"

Quotation #16

"*With* dawn, the sun rises again to *share* with us the *blessings* and *glory*. I feel calm *and* peace in my *mind* comparing *life* to *nature*."

Quotation #17

"*Words* are painful so do not *throw* them out *and* live to *regret*. Words are *powerful* too, so do *use* them as a *gift*."

Quotation #18

"*It* is true storms come, but it is also *true* that they *disappear* as *well*."

Quotation #19

"*May* we find in our heart, the *sparkling arrays* of love and *unite* all lands across the *globe*."

Quotation #20

"*Life* seems like a bowl of joy when you have everything. Again, to the other, it seems empty and lost as she has nothing. I see two sets of human prints on two sides of me. Looking at both, I say yes I have been there and I have gone past the joys and sorrows of life even though each moment seems like *eternity.*"

Quotation #21

"*When* all humans *unite*, even through *dark* times, all *obstacles* seem like ant hills not *Mount Everest*."

Quotation #22

"*Hope* is the only word we all look up to throughout this journey of life. Throughout the darkness, we hope for light as the darkness subsides. As the darkness fades away, we enter the door of light holding on to the hands of *hope*."

Quotation #23

"*Racism* is an *infectious* disease that *spreads* throughout the *lands*. These *days*, it is *infecting* even those of whom *we* *thought* to be *immune*."

Quotation #24

"*Dreams* are a form of *guidance* from The *Lord*."

Quotation #25

"*I* have complete faith
in The *Omnipotent*
and *believe* all
people *have* in
their *soul* the love for
The Omnipotent
as *well.*"

Quotation #26

"*Mother's* love endures all *pain* and lasts *forever*. May the *children* of *Earth* gather in *union* to *salute* and honor women of *Earth*."

Quotation #27

"*I* believe in
reincarnation, and
life is a circle,
but also believe this
life has been given
so we complete
the circle, not let
the circle complete us.
Change what has
been wronged
and not be
wronged."

Quotation #28

"*Love* is life's eternal *blessing*. *Love* is eternal *peace*, eternal *completeness*."

Quotation #29

"*Live* within your means. *Save* some *time* for the ones in *need*. Give the *gifts* of love and *time*."

Quotation #30

"*History* cannot be *changed*, but we can *learn* from the *past* and change the *future*."

Quotation #31

"*History* never *changes*. It is called history *because* it is the *past*. United we can change and *make history* again for the *future*."

Quotation #32

"*If* we place all *different* race, color, and *religion* together, *we* get the best *rainbow* on this *Earth*."

Quotation #33

"*The* complete inner *peace*, the awakening of the *soul*, reaches *beyond* the knowledge of *human mind*."

Quotation #34

"*Follow* your heart
and *know* even when
we are lost, *our*
mind, body, and
soul always show
and *guide* us to
the *truth*."

Quotation #35

"*Do* not become
a *stranger*,
be *yourself*.
It *is* then you
shall be *found*."

Quotation #36

"*Appreciation* breathes *energy* to *our* thirsty *soul*."

Quotation #37

"*Obstacles* are *teachers* of life, for when we *cross* them, *we* have *learned* our *lesson*."

Quotation #38

"*Let* us live life *together*, for in union *we* shall *overcome* all *obstacles*."

Quotation #39

"*We* the humans have grown up from *our* own *mistakes* and *achievements* because we *learn* from *history*."

Quotation #40

"*Remember* in every corner we *have* a *friend,* a *helping* hand whom *we* call *strangers.* I call them my *Angels.*"

Quotation #41

"*A* mother sees all *children* with the same *love*. A father *welcomes* all *children* with the same *heart*. I *love* all *humans* with my *soul*."

Quotation #42

"*Like* the rivers flow from one *land* to the other, they *change* names, *but* are the same body of *water*. May we spread *love* from one *heart* to the *other*."

Quotation #43

"*Love* heals *everything*. All the differences *are* *wiped* away through *love*."

Quotation #44

"*As* the days pass by, we know we *can* never *stop* time or tide, but we have *this* day, this *time*, so *today* *love* all of this around *us*."

Quotation #45

"*All* good deeds are a *sacred* spiritual *journey.*"

Quotation #46

"*It* matters not where you are in *your* life. It is what we do *with* It and *how* we *carry* ourselves throughout *our* *journey*."

Quotation #47

"*Life* is a test, live it as an *example* for *others* to be guided *by*."

Quotation #48

"*May* this year bring all creation *together* as one *world*. Above all race, color, *and* religion, is *love*. *Please* stop violence and spread *love*."

Quotation #49

"*Life* begins at birth, ends at *death*. It is called the *journey* of life. *Lord* keeps a *diary* of all the known *unknown*."

Quotation #50

"*Where* is the love?
In our *soul* is the
love. We spread it
one by *one.*"

Quotation #51

"*Life* begins as each one of us *awakens spiritually*. Let us *bring* this *spiritual* peace to *all*."

Quotation #52

"*May* the children create a *merciful bridge* of rainbow across all *lands* and unite all *humans*."

Quotation #53

"*Mother* Earth holds
on to *all* the memories
as they are *lost*
and *found*
throughout *time*."

Quotation #54

"*During* these dark nights, *we*, all race, color, *and* religion shall *unite* onto the *ark of faith*."

Quotation #55

"*Spiritual* journeys require no *traveling* but *unite* the soul to the *universe*."

Quotation #56

"*As* we move into the *future*, let us try *unitedly* to achieve the *positive* goals for all race, *color*, and *religion*."

Quotation #57

"*Let* us be the unifier in this time *and* space for it is *now* our *Earth* needs our *help*, for She has *given* us everything we *have*."

Quotation #58

"*We* have this day. As it has arrived at our door, it may leave joy, sorrow, or pain at our doorstep. We know tomorrow is peeking through the dark night's sky. As dawn breaks through, we shall have daylight *again*."

Quotation #59

"*Remember* the *future* is always *watching* you, for when the *future* *becomes* the *present*, it is then, *you* become *history*."

Quotation #60

"*Difference* between fear *and* spirituality is *personality.*"

Quotation #61

"*I* brought Mother Nature back into my *life* as my *guide*. She gives without *asking*. I had *taken* and never *thought* of her gift as a *gift*, but as a *guarantee*."

Quotation #62

"*I* know life is
like a *storm*,
completely *unique*,
as *sometimes*
we are given *notices*
and sometimes *it* just
happens."

Quotation #63

"*My* walk through the cave of *birth*, towards the cave of *death*, is but *blessed* for I *walk* with my *Lord*."

Quotation #64

"*The* difference *between* the beast and the *human* is basic moral *values*."

Quotation #65

"*Give* hope during the *dark* times and nights, for then let *us* be the *candle* bearer till *first* sight of *light*."

Quotation #66

"*Let* us build a bridge of *union* amongst all the *children* of *Mother* Earth as She *spills* the tears of *joy*."

Quotation #67

"*All* race, color, and religion, in *union* we are the *children*."

Quotation #68

"*The* hardest part about *standing* up against the *wrong* is *opening* the door and being *alone*."

Quotation #69

"*Reincarnation* came upon my *door* as the *memories* flooded *back*."

Quotation #70

"*Dreams* are another form *of* human *reincarnation.*"

Quotation #71

"*Through* dreams,
we get *Heavenly*
guidance."

Quotation #72

"*The* Angels of
The *Lord* pick us up
as we *fall* and place
us back on *track*."

Quotation #73

"*Growing* up does not mean *losing* all the *childish innocence*, for then I *would* rather not grow *up*."

Quotation #74

"Thought it was a *sacrifice*, but realized *it* is the spirit of my *life."*

Quotation #75

"*Love* is the complete *union* between The *Creator* and *creation*."

Quotation #76

"*Love* is for an artist capturing the *art* in his or her *frame*."

Quotation #77

"*Love* is watching the sunrise *and* sunset, *knowing* all of this is *free* for it belongs to The *Lord*."

Quotation #78

"*Life* is a gift from God. Let us *share* this *gift* with all through *kindness*, love, and *joy.*"

Quotation #79

"*Please* say a prayer, *asked* an elderly *mother*, a newlywed, and a *new* mother, as *I* went for a short morning *walk*."

Quotation #80

"*My* Lord, walk with us, so we are not *lost* in *grief*, loneliness, and *misery*."

Quotation #81

"*My* Lord, may we from all faith *find* You *amongst* us as we *hold* on to each *other*."

Quotation #82

"*Physical* pain *treated* through *medication,* *emotional* pain treated *through meditation.*"

Quotation #83

"*All* spiritual beings, let us *be* the *humanitarian bridge* between all *religions*."

Quotation #84

"*All* endeavors from our *past* become history *as* the *future* becomes the *present*."

Quotation #85

"*History* keeps an eye from the *future*, as the wheels of *time cross*, we the *present* become the *future*."

Quotation #86

"*Struggle* to stay *awake* during the dark *nights*? Know *dawn* is around the *corner*."

Quotation #87

"*Pouring* rain brings *calm* and peace to my heart, *for* it is then I *know* my Lord is sharing my *tears*."

Quotation #88

"*When* the sun sets, we have the *moon*. But *when* the moon sets, do not *lose* hope for then, *hold* on to the *twinkling* stars of *hope*."

Quotation #89

"*Hope* is our only way out from *being* lost. *Find* yourself first, *for* it is then you shall find *hope*."

Quotation #90

"*I* was asleep in my *human* body. It is then my *spiritual* soul but *awakened me.*"

Quotation #91

"*I* am the healer today *for* I was the *wounded yesterday*. *Unitedly* let us walk and heal *all tomorrow*."

Quotation #92

"*Journeyed* the road
of a *victim* first,
educated now.
Let us *be* the helping
hands for *others*."

Quotation #93

"*Physical* and *emotional* pain could not *knock* me *down* for I *love* my Lord more than *myself*."

Quotation #94

"*We* enter from the *unknown* and return to the *unknown*. It is our *journey* that separates *us*."

Quotation #95

"*Connection* between the *past* and the *future* is life's untold *journey*."

Quotation #96

"*A* walking stranger today, is *your friend* forever *tomorrow.*"

Quotation #97

"*A* child today, a *grandparent* tomorrow, yet *time* holds *still* as we wait *anxiously*."

Quotation #98

"*I* take help from my *dreams* as I get *lonely*. I remind myself, *dreams* are yet to be *true*."

Quotation #99

"*Nature* gives us lessons *from history*, yet we see *only* what we *want*."

Quotation #100

"*Face* of a school
filled *with* all race,
color, *and* religion,
is the *gift* of
The *Artist*,
The *Creator*."

Quotation #101

"*Blessings* are given from heart to *heart. Bless* all for before you *know* it, *blessings* shall knock on your *door.*"

Quotation #102

"*Peace* is just one beat away. *Touch* your heart and *find* it. Then, *be* the one to spread *it*."

Quotation #103

"*May* all the children of this world *find* peace *and* spread *peace*."

Quotation #104

"*Winter's* snow knocks on my *door*, so I have *lit* a candle for all. *Will* keep it *glowing* until the *sun's* ray blesses *all*."

Quotation #105

"*I* want to share the *tears* of every stranger. My *body* cries in pain, *please* no more. My *soul* *cries* out for she *wants* to share even *more*."

Quotation #106

"*Meditative* soul knows the *pure essence* of *meditation*."

Quotation #107

"*Moving* like wheels of a *wagon*, inspiration for *life* *comes* from the past *to* the present, inspiring the *future*."

Quotation #108

"*Let* history be there as a *guide*, but always create your *own* stories as we move *on* and become the *past*."

Quotation #109

"*As* all become the past and time *passes* by, let us *keep* the lights of *hope burning*, for *tomorrow* shall *arrive*."

Quotation #110

"*Be* the voice for those *who* do not *speak*, for those who do not *stand up* against violence, hunger, *or* struggles of *life*."

Quotation #111

"*Rainbows* of *sparkling* raindrops landed *upon* this Earth. *Love* spreads All *over* the lands, and as each *drop* awakens, *we* see *children*."

Quotation #112

"*At* all times, even when we are but *lost*, The *Lord* is *watching* over us *through* times of *sorrow* and during times of *joy*."

Quotation #113

"*I* know some have *family* and some do not, *but* at all times there are *some* around us *who* are more dear than *family*. I have *given* my mind, body, *and* soul *to* my *Lord*."

Quotation #114

"*Let* us not judge any one for we too *shall* be the *judged*. May we not be the *person* who we *love* to hate, but *let* us be the *one* we all *respect*, honor, and *love*."

Quotation #115

"*What* we do not have in the *pages* of *history* are the people who walk *around* each corner *and* have been *changing* the lives of so *many* throughout *time*."

Quotation #116

"*May* we the present spread this to the future and as they the future awaken and see the past, they shall know we have left onto them, the gift of love. May the future be blessed and may we the past be the reason for this blessed *future*."

Quotation #117

"*Life's* eternal gift is spiritual *freedom.*"

Quotation #118

"*Difference* between the *elderly* and the young is *time*."

Quotation #119

"*Share* the memories for with *time*, everything *is* lost but the *shared memories*."

Quotation #120

"*Moon* watches over all the *sweet dreams*, for even when *time* passes by, She keeps an *eye*."

Quotation #121

"*Depression* can only *weaken* the human *body*. Spiritual *awakening* strengthens the *mind*, body, and *soul*."

Quotation #122

"*Spiritual* awakening *holds* the *secret* to the unknown *worlds*."

Quotation #123

"*Endurance*
is achieved *as*
spiritual *awakening*
begins."

Quotation #124

"*Dreams* are a *form* of spiritual *awakening.*"

Quotation #125

"*Common* core
between the *traveler*
and the *bridge*
is the *journey*."

Quotation #126

"*Only* thing that remains still as time and tide move on is the memories framed in the hearts of the beholders. People change as does nature. Leaves fall off after giving us a glorious Fall of colors. New leaves bloom as Spring comes around again with new life blooming throughout this *universe.*"

Quotation #127

"*The* world
had taught me
everything as I walked
deep into my soul. I had
the realization of how
beautiful this world is.
It is like a Bridge of
Rainbow created by
different race, color,
and religion. Equally
beautiful and with
grace, each creation
is a unique sculpture,
a painting created by
The *Creator.*"

Quotation #128

"*My* rule is simple,
the *right* thing to do
and the *wrong*
thing to *avoid*."

Quotation #129

"*Whatever* path we *follow*, let peace, kindness, and *love* be our *guide*."

Quotation #130

"*As* tears flow, the voice of my inner *soul* says not what *could* have been, *but* what is, and that *we* have *survived*."

Quotation #131

"*The* world spreads herself like the *roots* of a banyan *tree* as she shelters *all* of her *children* into one *house*."

Quotation #132

"*Inspiration* is
the *struggles*,
the *obstacles*,
the *achievements*,
the endeavors of *life*."

Quotation #133

"*In* every teardrop and every *laugh*, there is a *lesson* which is *called* *inspirations* of *life.*"

Quotation #134

"*Inspiration* is not just the *lessons* of *life*, but the complete *journey* of *life*."

Quotation #135

"*Differences* were bridged through *love* and *created multicultural families.*"

Quotation #136

"*Sun's* glittering
ray brings *hope*
throughout the *day*.
With *nightfall*,
the *Sun* but
reincarnates as
the stars of *hope*,
never leaving *us*
for a *day*."

Quotation #137

"*Music* unites the *snake* and the snake *charmer*, as its rhythm *unites* the *world*."

Quotation #138

"*As* I was told growing up, all life eventually become stars in the dark skies to guide humans throughout the dark nights. So, my unknown friend shall become a guiding star for all humans. Tomorrow, another unknown friend shall be *born*."

Quotation #139

"*Powerful*
words again take me
through this dark night.
I know daylight comes
soon as The Lord's
blessings keep me
steadfast on my feet.
May all be protected
throughout the dark
nights. My faith is
strong and I know at
all times, it is

The Lord's *will*."

Quotation #140

"*Love*
all *without*
discrimination, *for* The
Lord created all and
loves all. Let us not
judge the creation
for we are *the* creation
who shall be *judged*
by The *Lord*.
Let there be *peace*."

Quotation #141

"*What* is unknown is a *mystery*, and some question, how *do* you love what is *not* known, or seen, *or heard* by the human ears? I *tell* them because I *love* you and all of *yours*."

Quotation #142

"*All* of these gifts on *Earth* were given to *us*, so you, I, and all *creation* live in *harmony*. These gifts were *created* and *given* by someone *who* loves, *gives*, and wants nothing in *return*."

Quotation #143

"*All* creation *are* scrambling around to find the *truth*, looking at all *doors* as they open *and* close. *For* all who seek, I tell *them* find yourself for *all* of the *knowledge* is in your *heart*."

Quotation #144

"*Do* not stress over this, for know this *life* on *Earth* is but a *day*."

Quotation #145

"*Spirituality,*
however you *call* and
however *you* see,
hear, or *ask*, it is the
complete *freedom*
from *all* negativity
and *joy* of all that
is *good.*"

Quotation #146

"*There* is someone in those shoes, *alone* walking *around* the corners *of* the sorrow *lane* or walking *and* skipping *around* the joyful victory *lane*."

Quotation #147

"*Sorrows* of life drown all *flooding* out the *memories*. Joys of life *drown* us *with* so much *energy* that we want to *live* in that time, day, *and* hour *forever*."

Quotation #148

"*Let* the crossroads be filled with *Angels* of *Mercy* who walk this Earth as *humans*, who *put* effort, *energy*, and time to look out for *all*."

Quotation #149

"*From* one heart to the other, *let* us bring *joy* and let us erase the *sorrow* from this world, *one* at a *time*."

Quotation #150

"*I* give you love
from the *inner* of
my *heart* which is the
only *gift* I can give,
and as we *share,*
it *grows.*"

Quotation #151

"*Let* us send positive energy *back* to this *world* through a *smile*, a kind word, a good *deed*, or like me *plant* a *tree* with all of your positive *energy*."

Quotation #152

"*May* we unite at
the *birth* of a child,
not just at the *door*
of *death*."

Quotation #153

"*I* know darkness comes *after* daylight, and it is the *truth* of life as *death* knocks on the *door* when our *time* on Earth is but *over*."

Quotation #154

"*We* shall triumph over evil *and victory* shall be for all *humans*, as we unite *against* all evil. *Let* religion not be the *focus*, but *union*, peace, and *blessings* flow from one *heart* to the *other*."

Quotation #155

"*In* union, all is but *created*. With *separation*, all is but *lost*."

Quotation #156

"*Healing* is strangers
holding on *to*
each other
for *support*."

Quotation #157

"*A* bridge created through the *support* of *strangers* is a blessed *dream*."

Quotation #158

"*Dreams* form
the *path* to
creativity."

Quotation #159

"*The* path is found
as the *search* is
completed."

Quotation #160

"*The* complete *truth* is a blessed *guide*."

Quotation #161

"*Eternal* blessings are *found* upon complete *giving*."

Quotation #162

"*Giving* is life's *complete journey*."

Quotation #163

"*Self-journey*
awakens the *soul*."

Quotation #164

"*The* soul travels throughout *eternity* to *find* peace and joy for *all*."

Quotation #165

ABOUT THE AUTHOR

I am an unknown person who lived the struggles, overcame the obstacles, as I have endured the pain and joy of life as they landed upon my door.

I like to be the unknown face to whom all can relate. I want you to see your face in the mirror when you search for me, not mine. For if it is my face in the mirror, then my friend you see a stranger. The unknown face is there so you see only yourself, your struggles, your achievements as you cross the journey of life. I want to be the face of a white, black, and brown, as well as the love we are always searching eternally for. If this world would have allowed, I would have distributed this inspirational quotation book to you with my own hands as a gift from a friend. Please take this book as a message from a friend.

You have my name and know I will always be there for anyone who seeks me. You can follow me @AnnahMariahRuby on Twitter, Ann Marie on my personal Facebook profile where the username is /annah.mariah.735, @TheAnnMarieRuby on my Facebook page, ann_marie_ruby on Instagram, and @TheAnnMarieRuby on Pinterest.

For more information about any one of my books, please visit my website www.annmarieruby.com.

I have published four books of original inspirational quotations:

> *Spiritual Travelers: Life's Journey From The Past To The Present For The Future*

> *Spiritual Messages: From A Bottle*

Spiritual Journey: Life's Eternal Blessings

Spiritual Inspirations: Sacred Words Of Wisdom

For all of you whom have requested my complete inspirational quotations, now I have for all of you, my complete ark of inspiration, I but call:

Spiritual Ark: The Enchanted Journey Of Timeless Quotations.

I have also published a book of original prayers:

Spiritual Songs: Letters From My Chest.

I am blessed to also share with you information about my upcoming book:

Spiritual Lighthouse: The Dream Diaries Of Ann Marie Ruby.

I give you a sample from my prayer book, *Spiritual Songs: Letters From My Chest* as I have written this book of prayers from my heart for all of whom seek the spiritual journey.

CANDLES OF HOPE

My Lord,

With the sun setting in Your vast sky,

The Earth but is in the dark.

May I, Your devotee,

Be there with a candle in my hand.

My Lord,

As the night sky but turns dark with

Your moon trying to peek through to give us hope,

May I, Your devotee,

Be there with a candle in my hand.

My Lord,

As house after house

But turns dark, searching for light,

May I, Your devotee, be the light bearer

With a candle in my hand.

My Lord,

As Your moon and twinkling stars

Try to send the message of Your sun's birth,

As all but watch out for the birth of Your sun,

May we, the creation,

Await and light up each house one by one

As we carry

The

CANDLES OF HOPE.

*From my prayer book, *Spiritual Songs: Letters From My Chest.*

My Spiritual Collection

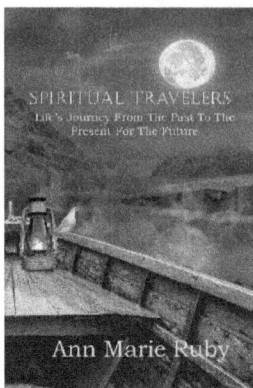

*Spiritual Travelers:
Life's Journey From
The Past To The Present
For The Future*

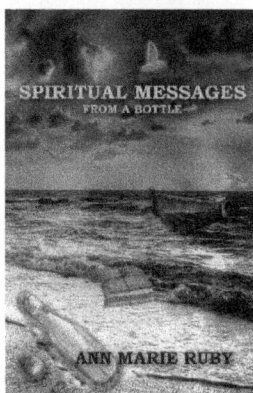

*Spiritual Messages:
From A Bottle*

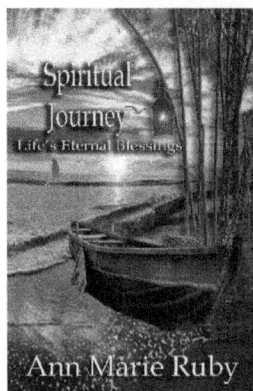

*Spiritual Journey:
Life's Eternal Blessings*

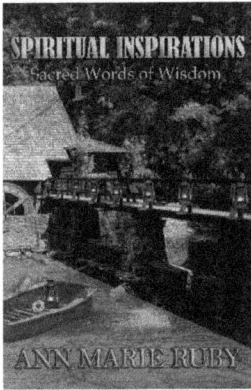

Spiritual Inspirations:
Sacred Words Of
Wisdom

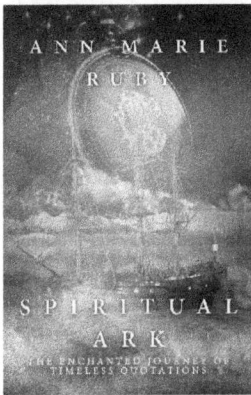

Spiritual Ark:
The Enchanted
Journey Of Timeless
Quotations

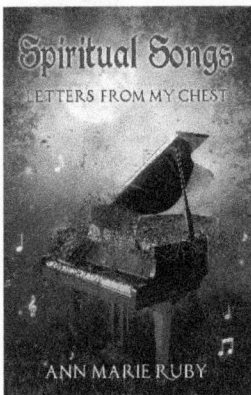

Spiritual Songs:
Letters From My Chest

My Upcoming Book

Spiritual Lighthouse:
The Dream Diaries Of Ann Marie Ruby

Within the dark, starless, foggy nights, my dreams appeared like the lighthouse always guiding me throughout my life. Dreams are spiritual guidance from the unknown. When the human body but falls asleep, it is then that our spiritual soul guides us throughout eternity. The soul walks into a parallel world where the past and the future exist in the same universe. Walk with me, as my soul but has walked the past and the future all throughout my life. Warnings, dangers, and surprises came upon my door, always guiding me like a lighthouse blinking in the dark night's sky. Alone, lost, and stranded I was until a lighthouse appeared within the ocean of the lost, my blessed dreams.

Take my hands and walk with me along this very personal path, as we journey together through my dream diaries, I call her, *Spiritual Lighthouse: The Dream Diaries Of Ann Marie Ruby*.

"Dreams are given from the Heavens above onto all within the Earth beneath for within them lie the miracles of eternity."

www.ingramcontent.com/pod-product-compliance
Lightning Source LLC
Chambersburg PA
CBHW031957040426
42448CB00006B/391